This notebook belongs to:

_____

_____

_____

'The knowledge of all things is possible.'
LEONARDO DA VINCI

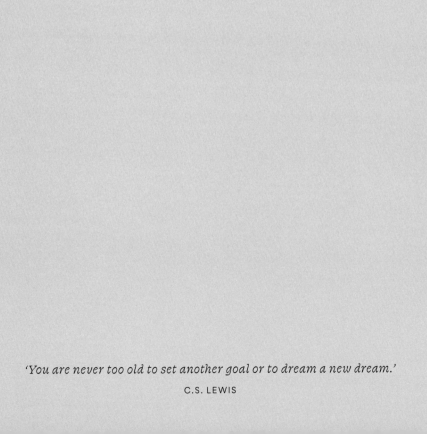

'You are never too old to set another goal or to dream a new dream.'

C.S. LEWIS

'You don't have to see the whole staircase, just take the first step.'
MARTIN LUTHER KING, JR.

'I dream my painting and I paint my dream.'
VINCENT VAN GOGH

'Even in dark times, we not only dream, we do.'

KAMALA HARRIS

Dreamer

Dreamer Mantra:
Live in the Moment

While they do have a *vision* for the future,
Dreamers prefer to take each day as it comes
and *focus* their attention on the *present*.
They tend to be more *impulsive* and *risk-taking*
than other personality types and go
by the general rule: *live first, think later.*

Personality Profile

*Imaginative * Aspiring * Intuitive*
*Curious * Philosophical*

Dreamers are highly imaginative and creative, characterised by their rich inner world and a love of storytelling – you will quickly spot a Dreamer at a party regaling a small crowd with a tale or intently listening to someone else's.

Dreamers are drawn to art, literature, music, culture and creative pursuits that energise and evoke strong emotions. A Dreamer is that person on a train who is completely engrossed in a book, being transported by one of their many themed Spotify playlists or captivated by a podcast.

Dreamers are highly empathetic people who are comfortable expressing emotion and like to connect with others in a deep and meaningful way. Often non-conformists, Dreamers reject convention and tradition in favour of the new and liberal. They typically experience emotional events and situations – such as a break-up or a political event – more strongly than others.

A laid-back, informal nature makes Dreamers easy friends and partners to have around – they bring a positive energy to all their relationships. Whether for a romantic partner or new friend, Dreamers fall quickly and deeply, readily clearing their schedule to spend lots of quality time getting to know the people who matter to them. They also have a tendency to 'go all in' too fast – after the initial high, they may find themselves bored and want to move on.

Champions of exhibiting and communicating emotions, they are quick to let their guard down and share feelings early on. Dreamers often draw on their intuition and self-reflection to connect with a partner or friend.

Dreamers have a strong intellectual curiosity – they love abstract ideas and exploring knowledge. A Dreamer will always prefer to rely on their own intuition and creativity than a tried-and-tested approach to a problem or task. They like to work at their own pace and juggle multiple things at the same time. This can often make them less planful, reliable and diligent when it comes to sticking to deadlines.

The Big Five Personality Traits

The 'Big Five' model was developed by psychologists in the field of personality science as a framework to describe human personality. The five broad traits outlined are: openness to experience, conscientiousness, extraversion, agreeableness and neuroticism – or 'OCEAN' for short.

Of all personality types, Dreamers score highest on the trait of **OPENNESS TO EXPERIENCE**. Personality researchers have found that people high in openness to experience see the world differently: they are more curious, expansive in their thinking, creative and imaginative. Openness reflects a tendency for individuals to be 'cognitive explorers' – deep thinkers who interrogate their own perceptions and emotions, and who are curious and investigative about ideas and philosophical arguments. In neuroscientific terms, a high level of openness to experience is associated with brain activity in the 'default network' – the neural system that is activated during experiences such as mind wandering and imagining other points of view.

CONSCIENTIOUSNESS refers to a tendency to be responsible, organised and hard-working. Those high in conscientiousness will exhibit more goal-oriented behaviour, meaning that when they make a plan or set a long-term goal, they usually stick to it. They also model good self-regulation and impulse control; for example, if they have an important task to finish, they are usually better at avoiding distraction or procrastinating. While Dreamers are on the spectrum of conscientiousness, they tend to score lower in this trait overall, preferring to go with the flow, be spontaneous and take a more laid-back approach to planning and discipline.

EXTRAVERSION refers to an individual's social energy and the conditions they need to recharge. In general, extraverts gain energy through interactions with people while introverts have less social energy and recharge by spending time alone or in solitude. It's important to remember that introversion is not to be confused with shyness – introverts are as sociable and people-loving as extraverts, they just need less stimulation and prefer smaller groups.

An introvert Dreamer is the friend you seek out when you need a listening ear, whether that be at two in the afternoon or two in the morning. They are sense-makers, highly perceptive and often take on a listening role. Introvert Dreamers enjoy new experiences but approach things in a more considered way than their extravert counterparts. Extravert Dreamers are more likely to be overt risk-takers and engage in daredevil activities.

AGREEABLENESS refers to an individual's preference for altruism and social harmony. Highly agreeable individuals are less 'me' and more 'we' and they may have a hard time saying no to others or going against the grain. Perceived to be friendly, optimistic and affectionate, people high in agreeableness tend to be empathetic, concerned for the welfare of others and more likely to help those in need. Dreamers can fall anywhere on the spectrum of agreeableness but tend to score higher than other personality types. Emotionally self-aware and adept at picking up social cues, Dreamers are likely to be in tune with their emotions and respond to others with empathy.

NEUROTICISM is associated with sensitivity to emotions, self-criticism and general anxiety. Those high in neuroticism tend to experience negative emotions more strongly than other personality types and therefore can be less even-tempered. High levels of neuroticism can also result in a more cynical outlook on life and being less comfortable in one's own skin. Again, Dreamers can fall anywhere on the spectrum of neuroticism, however, they may be susceptible to neurotic rumination as they are highly attuned to their own emotions and can become preoccupied with their own thoughts.

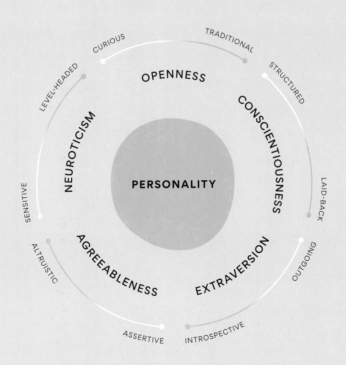

'A man, whilst
he is dreaming,
believes in his dream;
he is undeceived
only when he
is awakened from
his slumber.'

*

MAHATMA GANDHI

Super Powers

CURIOSITY

Dreamers are driven by curiosity both in pursuit of knowledge and in seeking out new experiences. Whether exploring a new subject area, reaching out to a new friend, freestyling a recipe or taking a new route into work, Dreamers are drawn to experience for experience's sake. As a Dreamer, when connecting with others, allow your natural curiosity to lead you to ask more open-ended questions to create space for deep and meaningful conversations rather than small talk.

CREATIVITY

Dreamers have a rich, colourful inner life that is a constant source of inspiration for them, sparking creativity and generating ideas. Dreamers perceive things deeply and have the capacity to consider things from multiple perspectives. Often, Dreamers are quite literally daydreamers, lost in their own imaginary world, reflecting on their day or absentmindedly people watching at a café. As a Dreamer, you frequently find yourself struck by new ideas – carry a notebook and be sure to write them down before they drift away.

EMOTIONAL AWARENESS

Dreamers spend a lot of time interrogating how they feel about something, whether that be a project they are working on or an interaction they have just had with someone. When it comes to making decisions, they are also more emotionally proactive and reactive than their friends. Dreamers aren't afraid to express how they feel. If a Dreamer experiences an emotional event or witnesses something that challenges their values, they will struggle to conceal their emotions. As a Dreamer, go with your gut when you are making important decisions.

ADVENTUROUSNESS

Dreamers are willing to take risks and try new things. Whatever Dreamers do, they are less likely to follow the norm or feel pressure to conform. A Dreamer may be a trailblazer among their peers – their clothing may stand out, they could be the first volunteer to try the spiciest dish on the menu or will convince friends to hike up a steep mountain trail to catch a sunrise when on holiday. As a Dreamer, embrace your audaciousness!

Dreamers think big and have vivid imaginations. Their creativity and vision set them apart. Whether envisioning a holiday or a project at work, Dreamers' imaginative optimism is infectious and draws people to them. At times, this optimism can tip towards being over-idealistic and Dreamers can subsequently become disappointed when reality does not match expectations. If you are a Dreamer who experiences this disappointment often, examine your expectations closely and ask yourself whether you are excited about the intrinsic value of what you are doing and the process of doing it or whether you are too focused on the outcome. Try to reset your expectations.

Growth Areas

TIME MANAGEMENT

As a Dreamer, time management is not really a strong suit! Dreamers spend much more time reflecting and thinking about a problem than planning or structuring an approach to solving it. This may cause Dreamers to miss important deadlines and create unnecessary stress for them and those around them. As a Dreamer, try to get into the habit of making to-do lists or breaking down big tasks into smaller chunks. If you know that you procrastinate, try tackling the hardest task first (and be sure to reward yourself afterwards!).

5 Things a Dreamer Should Have in Their Wallet

Mementos from their travels

Music, theatre (or musical theatre!) ticket stubs

Photographs of friends and family

Passport

Bookmark

INTROSPECTION

Dreamers like to reflect on their inner life – emotions, ideas, feelings, sense of purpose, where their passions lie and how they feel about their relationships. They may find themselves self-therapising after a difficult conversation or ruminating over how things could have gone differently. This can be helpful but also tiring! As a Dreamer, try ten minutes of free-writing before bed to help ensure you're not preoccupied with introspective thoughts at other times of the day.

DISCIPLINE

Dreamers are curious and love to try new things. This drive for novelty can lead a Dreamer to throw themselves into multiple tasks at once, taking on more and more projects and hobbies. A Dreamer may find they lack the discipline to stick with one thing in the long term or that they spread their energy too thinly. As a Dreamer, try building a practice of mindfulness to focus on one task at a time. One way to do this is to start your morning by writing down exactly what you want to achieve by the end of the day and, when those things are completed, reward yourself by doing something you really enjoy.

SENSITIVITY

Dreamers, particularly introvert Dreamers, are sensitive to their own and others' emotions. This can lead to deep and meaningful relationships but, at times, can also mean that Dreamers struggle to regulate their feelings and can take things to heart. Dreamers may also find themselves taking on too much and trying to fix things that are outside their control. It is a valuable skill to be able to tune into your own emotions and those of others; however, as a Dreamer, try to notice when you become preoccupied with these feelings and ensure that you limit the time you dedicate to this activity. Exercise self-compassion and try not to take the weight of the world on your shoulders.

DISTRACTION

As Dreamers have less of an inclination towards long-term planning and often entertain multiple thoughts at once, they can be easily distracted and may find it hard to focus on a single task. As a Dreamer, when you sit down to an important task, try to remove as many distractions as possible. Start where it hurts and minimise distractions from your phone: if WhatsApp notifications drain your focus, mute them or, better yet, put your phone on flight mode. Help restore a feeling of quiet and increase your level of focus. Give yourself permission to enjoy distraction but do it intentionally – ideally as a reward for a burst of focus.

Dreamer Rituals and Habits

MAKE EVERY DAY DIFFERENT

More than any other personality type, Dreamers would rather mix it up than play it safe: surprise and variety make a Dreamer feel alive. Dreamers love to make last-minute plans with a friend on a Wednesday evening or break routine and get out of bed at a different time every day. As a Dreamer, if life feels stagnant, challenge yourself to make every day a little bit different: it can be as small as eggs cooked in a different way or new lock-screen wallpaper.

BE SPONTANEOUS

Dreamers like to have a spontaneous existence – they prefer to have unstructured time in their day where they get to choose what to do. This might be playing their record collection, listening to a podcast while folding the laundry, staring out of the window or going for a walk without a plan. Challenge yourself to leave free space in your schedule and embrace one spontaneous activity every weekend – see how you feel!

JOURNAL BEFORE BED

Dreamers often have a head full of thoughts after a long day. To calm a busy mind, try journaling before bed. Don't worry about structuring your thoughts – the most important thing is to keep writing. If you've never journaled before, start with five minutes each night and increase the time depending on how you feel.

AVOID A UNIFORM

You may have some wardrobe staples but try to avoid wearing the same thing every day. If you don't normally wear colour, try it! As a Dreamer, a pop of yellow or red on a Monday morning may be just the thing you need to boost your mood or inspire a new idea.

UNWIND YOUR MIND

For every personality type, it's important to find a pursuit that calms your mind. As a Dreamer, routine can be agitating, so find a few different habits that reduce your stress levels. It could be as simple as bringing mindfulness to chopping an onion for dinner, making time for a weekly walk with a friend, meditating or, as a thinker, finding a hobby that means you work with your hands.

'The only limit to
the height of your
achievements
is the reach of your
dreams and your
willingness to work
hard for them.'

*

MICHELLE OBAMA

Compatibility

WHO DO YOU CONNECT WITH?

Dreamers attach huge importance to their friends and family and surround themselves with people with whom they see eye to eye. They have an eclectic group of friends and particularly value close one-on-one relationships.

Dreamers are often drawn to fellow Dreamers – friends who listen intently, embrace spontaneity and are happy to skip small talk. That's not to say that Dreamers only connect with other Dreamers – they value different personality types and relish the opportunity to hear stories and learn from others of different backgrounds and inclinations.

WHO MIGHT YOU CLASH WITH?

Dreamers are strong communicators who empathise easily. It can, therefore, be difficult for a Dreamer to relate to someone who is less emotionally aware and socially fluent, less in tune with people around them. As Dreamers are guided by their emotions, they will often find it frustrating to be confronted with pure rationality, logic and pragmatism. Dreamers go with the flow and actively seek out experiences that are outside the ordinary – they are drawn to the unusual. As a result, Dreamers are usually at odds with traditionalists who prefer the conventional over the new. As a Dreamer, therefore, you are likely to find it difficult to work with those who stick to an established path and you might want to avoid being picked for the same assignment. If you do find yourself on the same team, try to schedule a conversation early on to discuss your different working styles.

5 Things You Should Never Say/Do to a Dreamer

Make plans with a Dreamer without their diary

Tell a Dreamer to follow the 'tried and tested' method

Take a Dreamer on a sightseeing bus in a new city

Schedule back-to-back meetings

Answer only 'yes' or 'no' to their questions

WHO DO YOU WORK WELL WITH?

Although Dreamers clash with the working style of more traditionalist doers, they often do their best work when balanced by someone who can take the lead when it comes to more structured tasks, such as planning, working towards goals and paying close attention to detail. Dreamers are thinkers, revelling in reflection, and are rarely long-term planners. Finding the right balance between a Dreamer approach and doers who have a strong sense of discipline and the ability to work towards goals can be the foundation of a strong partnership.

WHO DO YOU HAVE A SECRET CRUSH ON?

As Dreamers score highly in openness to experience they are less likely to have a specific romantic 'type' and are open to a range of different people. Dreamers will crush on those with whom they feel a more abstract connection and potential for meaningful conversation, whether it be a stranger at a party or a friend that could turn into something more.

WHO DO YOU WISH YOU WERE MORE LIKE?

Defining a Dreamer's aspirational or influential figure is tricky as they tend to have wide-ranging interests spanning, for instance, art, music, film and philosophy. However, a running theme is that Dreamers aspire to be someone who embodies creativity and imagination but also has the drive and vision to follow through on those plans. A Dreamer's role models are self-reflective, creative individuals with the discipline and focus to turn big ideas and abstract concepts into reality. Typically, these are creative entrepreneurs, artists, people who live their passions, game-changers, visionaries and pioneers in all fields.

5 Things a Dreamer Will Say

'Let's play it by ear'

'Of course we have time'

'Happy to go with the flow'

'Time to go back to the drawing board'

'Let's try all of them'

In Friendships and Family

DREAMERS BRING OPTIMISM

Dreamers bring a positive energy to any interaction and are well liked. Dreamers are more likely to have a diverse friendship group than other personality types. They have friends from every life stage – childhood, university, work and the random friendships they've struck up at their local café or gym. They have a laid-back attitude and don't get bogged down by details or planning. They prefer to live in the here and now and have a magnetic presence in any friend group.

DREAMERS VALUE ACCEPTANCE

Compared to other personality types, Dreamers are less rigid and more relaxed. Dreamers have one of the most laid-back familial styles – creating a warm, open-minded environment. Dreamers tend not to shy away from fear of failure and instead embrace the mistakes that inevitably take place. A Dreamer will accept you as you are and expect the same in return.

DREAMERS NEED QUALITY TIME

When hosting a party, a Dreamer is likely to bring together a motley crew. However, with each set of friends, Dreamers value quality time rather than surface-level conversations. Dreamers need an emotional investment in their relationships as it gives them a sense of purpose. They prefer to spend uninterrupted time with friends and family, and love the idea of a holiday without phones and distractions.

DREAMERS NEED TO SHARE EXPERIENCES

As Dreamers are deeply spontaneous and adventurous, they revel in making memories with their friends and family. Whether it be a casual Sunday dinner or road trips and travel, every experience is an opportunity to bond.

DREAMERS LOVE PLAYTIME

Dreamers are likely to pursue a wide range of hobbies and activities and enjoy sharing their passions with friends and family. Dreamers will actively fill their social calendars with new activities: a pop-up restaurant, an exhibition, a walk through an unknown part of the city. Travel is also an important pastime for a Dreamer and finding friends who share their love for adventure is high on a Dreamer's wish list.

In Romantic Relationships

DREAMERS VALUE EMOTIONAL EXPRESSION

In a romantic relationship, Dreamers prize emotional expression and connection over material gifts or grand gestures. They value affirmation and like to say and do things to make their partner feel seen, heard and appreciated, and to receive that in return. (Extra points if it's spontaneous!) Dreamers feel particularly valued when a partner takes time to thoughtfully reflect and comment on something positive they have noticed them doing.

DREAMERS ARE ROMANTICS

Dreamers are the ultimate romantics – they have vivid imaginations and, often, abstract notions of love. Dreamers are inspired by almost all kinds of love stories, high and low, from sonnets to rom-coms. Romantic gestures such as impromptu dates, unexpected flowers and handwritten letters form a big part of Dreamers' love language.

DREAMERS ARE EMOTIONALLY AWARE

Dreamers experience more, and more intense, emotional states than other personality types. In a relationship, introvert Dreamers are particularly emotionally clued-up and sensitive – they pick up on emotional cues and are in tune with their partner's emotions. This can lead to a meaningful bond based on emotional safety and comfort.

Extravert dreamers are less emotionally sensitive than introvert dreamers but are highly expressive when it comes to their emotions. In the heady days of early-stage romance, extravert dreamers need to make their emotions and feelings known, which can make them magnetic romantic partners.

DREAMERS FOLLOW THEIR HEART

Dreamers typically make decisions based on emotions and gut instinct. When weighing up whether to enter a relationship, Dreamers are likely to focus on how it makes them feel above any other consideration. Despite Dreamers' ability to go with the flow, given their high emotional awareness, they may find themselves checking the pulse of a relationship a little too often – requesting regular conversations about how both partners feel and, at times, creating the kind of relational stress that keeps both parties awake at night!

For both introvert and extravert Dreamers, sharing common interests is an important foundation to the success of a relationship. Dreamers are strongly drawn to arts and culture, so a partner who shares this is ideal. At the same time, Dreamers are driven by curiosity, so seek out people who expand their horizons and take them beyond their current interests.

Dreamers at Work

DREAMERS' DREAM JOB AND WORK ENVIRONMENT

Dreamers are typically drawn to professions in creative industries. They thrive in pursuits that allow them to express themselves and bring their imagination, aesthetic sense and rich inner life to the table. They are typically ill-suited to repetitive or rote positions as they are always thinking up new ways to do things. Dreamers adapt well to uncertainty – they don't need a structured plan for every task; in fact, they often do their best work without one. Dreamers thrive in an environment that is flexible and provides autonomy. When in non-creative professions, Dreamers often have side hustles or hobbies that allow them to express themselves outside their professional life. Dreamers excel in teams and open-plan office settings – the idea of working in complete solitude strikes fear in their hearts.

DREAMERS FAIL FAST

At work, Dreamers are less likely to focus on perfection than on pushing themselves out of their comfort zone and exploring uncharted territory. For a Dreamer, the motto 'Fail fast' is much more likely to be stuck to their desk than 'Practice makes perfect'. In leadership roles, Dreamers strive to create a culture where their colleagues feel agency and where freedom of expression is encouraged.

5 Dream Jobs for a Dreamer

Graphic designer   Artist   Copywriter   Teacher   Advertising executive

DREAMERS ARE CREATIVE THINKERS

Dreamers like to think outside the box and will be the first to dive into the process of generating ideas, believing, at least initially, that there are no bad ones and the bigger, the better. This approach ensures their colleagues don't get too bogged down in the details. Visual aids such as Post-it notes, highlighters and coloured index stickers may help Dreamers when brainstorming and visualising.

DREAMERS ARE HUNGRY TO LEARN

Dreamers are driven to engage deeply with ideas and concepts, and having time to reflect, theorise and learn is something Dreamers care about at work. Dreamers like to learn for the sake of learning, rather than to reach a particular outcome. When Dreamers latch onto a concept or idea that they feel passionate about, they are not afraid to show this passion or pursue it – and this is often infectious. Although less analytical than other personality types, Dreamers often spot seemingly random connections that others don't due to their ability to zoom out and see a bigger picture.

DREAMERS QUESTION EVERYTHING

Dreamers are often the ones asking questions at a team meeting or, if introvert, noting them down to follow up later, and they can be assertive when they need to be! Dreamers are valuable to a team as they don't take things for granted; instead, they probe important assumptions and consider alternatives to the status quo.

At Play

DREAMERS INDULGE IN THE ARTS

Dreamers live and breathe culture, art and other creative stimuli. As a Dreamer, be sure to continue to invest your time and resources in these pursuits.

DREAMERS EXPLORE THEIR CREATIVITY

A Dreamer will often have multiple hobbies and projects on the go. An ideal activity for a Dreamer is one that is novel, engaging and fulfils their need for creative expression. This could be something like a pottery or life-drawing class or, if a more extravert Dreamer, something like basketball or a trampolining class. Even spending the afternoon at a local vintage shop satisfies a Dreamer's need to explore and try new things.

'The important
thing is not to
stop questioning.
Curiosity has
its own reason
for existing.'

*

ALBERT EINSTEIN

DREAMERS GO OFF PISTE

Dreamers live to travel and immerse themselves in new cultures and contexts. For a Dreamer, travel is more about atmosphere and experiences than checking off a list of tourist sites. A Dreamer might pack a Lonely Planet guide but, when in Rome, for example, they are likely to ditch the Colosseum in favour of striking up conversation with locals or wandering along cobbled streets, creating memories.

DREAMERS GET OUT IN NATURE

Dreamers are often the first to suggest getting away into nature (although less likely to want to plan it!). Dreamers love fresh air and wilderness away from the city and use time in nature to be reflective and renew themselves. Given Dreamers' love of novelty, excursions into nature may also feature a new activity, such as following literary landmarks in the area, kite boarding, zip-lining or trying out a new camera.

DREAMERS BELIEVE IN ACTIVISM

Dreamers genuinely believe that ideas make a difference. When a Dreamer latches onto an idea or a social issue they care about, they are deeply passionate about it. Although Dreamers are generally relaxed and can compartmentalise this passion, their positive energy for change is infectious wherever they take it.

5 New Hobbies for a Dreamer

Cooking   Photography   Journaling

Interior decorating   Dance

Dreamers and Self-Care

ME TIME

Dreamers, especially introvert Dreamers, can only fully unwind when they have time to themselves to reflect and recharge. This could be as simple as taking a long shower or scheduling an afternoon of unstructured time to fully immerse themselves in their own thoughts. As a Dreamer, just remember that 'me time' doesn't necessarily mean not seeing other people – staying in touch with others is an important part of your wellbeing and it might be more about seeing people on your own terms.

DIGITAL DETOX

As a Dreamer, too much social media may sap your creative energy. Try a digital detox from social media for a day, if that feels good. Put your phone on flight mode, leave it in another room or designate a specific time to check it – there's no hard or fast rule. Do whatever feels right to get a sense of balance back into your day.

EXERCISE

We know that exercise is a huge boost for wellbeing. For more extravert Dreamers, a high-tempo gym class or a run accompanied by a favourite playlist may do the trick. For introvert Dreamers, activities such as yoga and barre can provide the slow-down and space for mindfulness that is needed.

SHAKE UP YOUR ROUTINE

Dreamers are not creatures of habit – repetition can even be a source of stress! If you're feeling a sense of inertia, boredom or tension, try mixing up your routine.

PRIORITISE A HEALTHY WORK-LIFE BALANCE

If Dreamers overexert themselves at work, they are likely to feel a ripple effect on their wellbeing. While Dreamers love nothing more than to work hard on something they feel passionate about, down time and the opportunity to indulge in their own interests is pivotal to a Dreamer's wellbeing. As a Dreamer, if you feel like you're not getting enough 'you time' in a week, block out a specific time in advance, even if it's a half an hour every day to take a walk in the park.